MIKE YOUNG

SUPERTED AND THE STOLEN ROCKET SHIP

Illustrations by Tony Hutchings

Frederick Muller Limited
London

SuperTed and Spottyman have been invited by a famous scientist to watch the launch of the world's latest rocketship. Three astronauts will travel deeper into space than any man has ever been before.

The scientist points at the astronauts, 'Those brave men will fly to the planets of the Milky Way.'

'Milky Way? I went there for my summer holidays,' exclaimed Spottyman.

'Spotty, Shh . . .,' whispered SuperTed.

'There go the astronauts making their way to the capsule,' said the scientist.

'Mmm, I wonder?' thought a puzzled SuperTed.

Meanwhile, behind the launch pad those villains Bulk, Skeleton and Texas Pete, have captured the astronauts and stolen their spacesuits.

'Ha! Ha! See, I told you becoming an astronaut is as easy as falling off a log,' laughed Texas Pete.

Skeleton is, as usual, worried, 'I think we should go back, I don't think we've had the right training for this kind of thing.'

Tex is annoyed, 'What do you mean, I trained you, didn't I?'

'Yes, but only to rob a bank!' moaned Skeleton.

From the control room everything looks normal. The countdown begins: 10,9,8,7,6,5,4,3,2,1, we have lift off!

As the rocket speeds into the sky, SuperTed looks worried. 'I don't like it Spotty . . . there was something funny about those spacesuits. I know what it was! They didn't fit properly. Quick Spotty, let's go!'

The chums find the astronauts tied up with rattlesnakes and shaking with fear.

As SuperTed untied the snakes, he said, 'You see, if you're kind to them they won't hurt you.'

'Gee thanks . . . saved by a teddy bear,' said the astronaut.

'There's only one person who would tie people up with a rattlesnake . . . Texas Pete. Hm . . . I'll say my magic word.' Whoosh — the teddy bear changes into SuperTed. 'We'll use your rocket, Spotty.'

'Yes,' replied the proud Spottyman. 'It's the only one fast enough to catch them.'

Thousands of miles away, all is quiet in the stolen rocket. Texas Pete, Bulk and Skeleton are all fast asleep. Tex begins to dream . . . *'I'm Texas Pete, ruler of the universe. I'll round up every planet and have it branded with my name in big letters! I'll be more famous then Billy the Kid!'*

Suddenly he wakes up to find himself in mid air. 'Hey we're floating!'

Bulk's nose hits a red button. 'Ouch!' he moans and the rocket speeds off out of control.

TEX
TEX
TEX
TEX
TEX
TEX

Speeding through space in the Spottyship, SuperTed and Spottyman look carefully at the radar screen.

'I can't see anything but spots,' said the confused Teddy.

'Look! There they are,' pointed Spotty. 'It's jumping around like an excited pony.'

'Right Spotty, let's get after them.'

Still floating helplessly inside the spacecraft, the villains struggle to regain control. Tex is clinging to a chair, 'Get off my leg Skeleton. You're pulling down my pants.'

'But I've got nothing else to hold on to.'

Bulk, looking out of the window, upside down, sees the Spotty spaceship.

'Tex, look at that lovely rocket out there.'

Just at that moment they collide with a small meteor. Their spaceship is damaged.

Tex shouts, 'You idiots! Get out there and stick those bits back on.'

Bulk and Skeleton float through the hatch outside the spacecraft.

'This is great,' shouts the stupid Bulk, 'I can fly.'

All of a sudden they hear a whoosh, it's the Spotty spaceship. 'Oh no,' they chorus, 'Not that terrible teddy!'

The Spotty ship collides with Skeleton, puncturing his suit. 'Ooow,' squeals Skeleton, 'I can't move a muscle . . . not surprising, I haven't got any muscles. Boo hoo hoo!' he begins to cry.

SuperTed, his rocket boots on full power, zooms at Bulk. 'Your turn next, Bulk!'

He breaks the air tube to Bulk's spacesuit and blows up the suit like a balloon.

'Don't, you mustn't!' shouts Bulk. SuperTed lets go and the unfortunate Bulk speeds, zig-zagging, through space.

Texas Pete, still in his stolen rocket, starts up the motor to make his escape, and blasts SuperTed with the rocket exhaust and flames. The brave teddy is sent spinning head over heels.

Spottyman races across to him. 'SuperTed, are you all right? Wake up, you'll have to stop him or he'll cause chaos across the cosmos.'

SuperTed is a bit giddy.

'I'm all right, just knocked a bit of the stuffing out of me. Bubbling Blancmange, where's Texas Pete, we must go after him. Come on!'

Meanwhile, Texas Pete has a wicked idea, 'Look, there's that Spotty rocketship, I'll ram it out of existence. Then they'll never get home again.'

Spottyman shouts a warning, 'Look, he's going to ram my lovely rocket. Get him SuperTed!'

SuperTed speeds to the stolen rocket,and clinging on desperately,uses all his strength to bend open the hatch and dive inside.

'Get your nasty paws off me,you horrid little teddy bear!' warns Texas Pete.

'Don't toy around with me, Texas. Take that!' SuperTed hits Texas Pete on the head with his paw,and the silly baddie's head spins round until he thinks he's seeing stars.

Later, back at the rocket base . . .

'Well, goodbye SuperTed and Spottyman, and thank you. Don't worry about the villains, we'll take care of them.'

'Goodbye,' waved the chums, as they climbed into the Spotty rocketship.

'You were right about one thing, Spotty.'
'What?'
'Your rocketship. It can knock spots off anything we've got on Earth.'